W9-CIG-161

MULTICULTURAL
LITERATURE

A READER'S GUIDE TO
CHINUA ACHEBE'S

# Things Fall Apart

## GEORGE SHEA

**Enslow Publishers, Inc.**
40 Industrial Road
Box 398
Berkeley Heights, NJ 07922
USA
http://www.enslow.com

## Acknowledgement

The author wishes to express his appreciation to Martha Stevens for her many generous and valuable contributions to this book.

*To Martha Stevens—with deep gratitude and affection.*

Copyright © 2008 by George Shea

All rights reserved.

No part of this book may be reproduced by any means without the written permission of the publisher.

### Library of Congress Cataloging-in-Publication Data

Shea, George.
  A reader's guide to Chinua Achebe's Things fall apart / George Shea.
    p. cm. — (Multicultural literature)
  Includes bibliographical references and index.
  ISBN-13: 978-0-7660-2831-9
  ISBN-10: 0-7660-2831-3
  1. Achebe, Chinua. Things fall apart—Juvenile literature.  I. Title.
  PR9387.9.A3T5368 2007
  823'.914—dc22

                              2006038486


Printed in the United States of America
10 9 8 7 6 5 4 3 2 1

Supports the English/Language Arts and Literature curricula

**To Our Readers:**
We have done our best to make sure all Internet addresses in this book were active and appropriate when we went to press. However, the author and the publisher have no control over and assume no liability for the material available on those Internet sites or on other Web sites they may link to. Any comments or suggestions can be sent by e-mail to comments@enslow.com or to the address on the back cover.

**Illustration Credits:** AP/ Wide World Photos, pp. 17, 109; Courtesy of Western Michigan University, pp. 27, 34, 53, 68; Enslow Publishers, Inc., p. 23; Time & Life Pictures/ Getty Images, p. 4.

**Cover Illustration:** Jupiterimages Corporation.

# Contents

Author Chinua Achebe displays two editions of his famous novel *Things Fall Apart* in this publicity photo taken in 1960.

# CHAPTER 1

# An African Novel

Chinua Achebe was intensely angry with the book his white English college professor had assigned him to read. The year was 1953, and Achebe was one of a handful of brilliant young African students attending University College in Nigeria.

Achebe's professor had recommended the book to his class as an excellent example of an "African novel." The book was *Mister Johnson* and its author was Joyce Cary, an Anglo-Irish writer who had served in Nigeria between 1913 and 1920 as an assistant district officer and also as an officer in the British army in Cameroon. Cary's novel had received much critical acclaim in England.

The most upsetting passage of all for Achebe was that in which Cary described the fictitious Nigerian village where *Mister Johnson* takes place:

> *Fada is the ordinary native town of the Western Sudan. It has no beauty, convenience or health. It is a dwelling-place at one stage from the rabbit warren or badger burrow; and not so cleanly kept as the latter. It is a pioneer settlement five or six hundred years old, built on its own rubbish heaps, without charm even of antiquity. Its squalor and its stinks are all new . . . All its mud walls are eaten as if by smallpox; half of the mats in any compound are always rotten. Poverty and ignorance, the absolute government of jealous savages, conservative as only the savage can be, have kept it at the first frontier of civilization.*[1]

The main character in Cary's book is a childlike, empty-headed, irresponsible, free-spirited young African named Mister Johnson. Johnson has lucked into a job as clerk to Rudbeck, the British district commissioner: a shy, duty-driven, British civil servant. Johnson owes money all over the district, and has also been helping himself to funds from the local treasury using the money to throw big noisy parties for his friends. The fun fades when Johnson is confronted by an angry group of local people who come after him demanding the money he owes them:

> Johnson puts down his head and rushes past her into the clerk's office, where he collapses into a chair. He rolls up his eyes to the roof and mutters, "Oh, Gawd! Oh, Jesus! I done finish—I finish now—Mister Johnson done finish— Oh, Gawd, you no fit do nutting—Mister Johnson too big damn fool—he fool chile—oh, my Gawd." He hits himself on the forehead with his fist. "Why you so bloody big dam' fool, you Johnson?[2]

Years later in an autobiographical reflection in *Home and Exile*, Achebe recalled his class's reaction to the book. One of his classmates stood up and told an astounded teacher that the only moment he enjoyed in the entire book was when the Nigerian "hero," Johnson, was shot to death by his British master, Rudbeck. "The rest of us," Achebe recalled, "now astounded too, offered a medley of noises in reaction . . . we all shared our colleague's exasperation at this bumbling idiot of a character whom Joyce Cary and our teacher were so assiduously passing off as a poet when he was nothing but an embarrassing nitwit!"[3]

Achebe recalled the incident as "more than just an interesting episode in a colonial classroom."

> *It was a landmark rebellion. Here was a whole class of young Nigerian students, among the brightest of their generation, united in their view of a book of English fiction in complete opposition to their English teacher, who was moreover backed by the authority of metropolitan critical judgement. The issue was not so much who was right as why there was that absolute divide.*[4]

Achebe came of age at a time when young Africans were opposing European rule through political action and questioning the cultural assumptions Europeans used to justify that rule.

Like many other young Nigerians of his generation, Achebe was given a standard British education with a college syllabus that included Shakespeare, Milton, Wordsworth, and Dickens. It also included novels set in Africa by more contemporary, twentieth-century, white, European writers such as Joseph Conrad, Graham Greene, and Joyce Cary. These were books that described the African experience in a purely colonial context, regarding it strictly from the point of view and experience of the white European settler.

In an interview with fellow African writer, Lewis Nkosi, about his college days, Achebe said of *Mister Johnson*, "It was clear to me that it was a most superficial picture of—not only of the country—but even of the Nigerian character. And so I thought if this was famous, then someone ought to try and look at this from the inside."[5]

The result was the most famous and influential novel ever written about Africa, *Things Fall Apart*. Today, *Things Fall Apart* is recognized as a literary classic and is taught and read everywhere in the English-speaking world. The novel has also been translated into fifty languages, and has sold 10 million copies. Its author was Chinua Achebe.

Achebe was born in the village of Ogidi in Igboland in eastern Nigeria on November 16, 1930. Until he was eight years old, young Albert (as he was originally named) spoke only Igbo and grew up learning Igbo folk stories at his mother's knee. That same year, he was sent to the local Anglican school, St. Philip's Central School, to learn English. Thus, he grew up with one foot in the ancient oral Igbo storytelling tradition and the other in modern English literature.

Young Achebe excelled at school, and when he was thirteen he gained entrance to the prestigious Government College, Umuahia. The decision to attend Government College was probably made by Albert's older brother, John, who had taken over the boy's training. Government College was free of missionary control and proudly displayed as its crest a pair of torches, one black and one white, shining together.

After Achebe graduated with high honors, he was one of a highly select number of young Nigerians chosen for admission to the new University College at Ibadan. The college had a direct relationship with the University of London and aimed to become one of the best higher education institutions in Africa.

Expectations ran high that it would be from among its graduates that the future leaders of an independent Nigeria would emerge. Talk of independence for Britain's African colonies was very much in the air as Achebe headed off for Ibadan.

His older brother John, now his official guardian, decided he should study medicine, so young Achebe passed an unhappy, grinding freshman year studying physics and medicine, two subjects that did not really interest him. In the meantime, as he later recalled, there were stories in his head he wanted to tell that "just wouldn't let me go."[6]

At the end of the year, Achebe went to the school's administration and told them he wanted to switch his major to English, geography, and history. It was a decision that meant he would lose his scholarship.

Achebe made another major decision that same year when he gave up his Christian European name of Albert and adopted the Igbo name of Chinua. A new scholarship was awarded to him after his second year. He excelled in his studies and began to write short stories. After he graduated in 1953, he worked for several months as a teacher in a small rural high school and then received an offer to work for the Nigerian Broadcasting Service (NBS) as director of its radio *Talks* program.

This was an important post. The British Colonial Administration that ran Nigeria was aware that, with the coming of independence, British broadcasters would be leaving and capable Nigerians would be needed to take their places. Achebe's radio job put him in Lagos, Nigeria's future capital and the center of the country's social and political activity. The job enabled him to view political, social, and economic events up close as his department played a key role in assembling and disseminating information on political developments in Nigeria.

Achebe very soon showed he was more than ready when he did an impressive job of handling his first story production assignment. He had an excellent ear for dialogue, for expressing naturally the way people talked in their everyday lives. For a future novelist, radio reporting was an invaluable experience that put him in contact with a great variety of people at a very exciting and pivotal time in Nigeria's (and Africa's) history.

In 1956, Achebe accepted an invitation to go to London and study broadcasting techniques at the BBC Staff School. He had already started writing a novel and wanted it to be one "which would reflect some of his reactions to the social and political issues confronted by his culture."[7]

There were no models upon which to construct an African novel since modern African fiction in English barely existed. Only two

African-written novels had ever been published, Amos Tutuola's *The Palm-Wine Drinkard* in 1952 and Cyprian Ekwensi's *People of the City* in 1954. African fiction in Nigeria was still an oral tradition in which stories were spoken and passed on from one generation to the next.

By the end of March 1956, Achebe had completed a first draft of the novel to which he gave the tentative title, *Things Fall Apart*. It was accepted for publication in 1958. It received quick and highly enthusiastic reviews in the British press and a year later, it won the distinguished Margaret Wrong Prize, named for an English missionary who promoted literary activities in East Africa.

On October 1, 1960, Nigeria became a nation, officially receiving its independence from Great Britain. That same year Achebe's second novel, *No Longer at Ease*, was published. By then Achebe, still employed at the NBS in Lagos, had met a young female employee and technology college graduate, Christie Chinwe Okoli. Chinua and Christie were married in September 1961.

A month later, *No Longer at Ease* won the Nigerian National Trophy for Literature, an award created to mark the first anniversary of Nigerian independence. Other novels soon followed, including *Arrow of God* (which some critics consider his best) in 1964.

Achebe's radio career was cut short in 1966 by a series of violent political events. Nigeria as a nation was composed of three different regions dominated by the principal ethnic groups in the country: the Hausa and Fulani in the north; the Yoruba in the southwest; and the Igbo (also called the Ibo, though Igbo is regarded as the more acceptable or correct spelling today) in the southeast. In 1966, a military coup toppled Nigeria's democratically elected, but highly corrupt, government. As the economic situation worsened, ethnic violence broke out. Up to thirty thousand Igbos were killed, many of them massacred by the Hausas, while another million were forced to flee to their Igbo homeland in the east.

In May 1967, Igbo leaders declared eastern Nigeria independent from Nigeria and the independent republic of Biafra was proclaimed. The Nigerian government opposed the secession and attacked Biafra. It was a very uneven contest since the Nigerian armed forces had the advantage of overwhelming military aid from Britain. Over two and a half years later, a million Igbos died in the fighting and from starvation caused by the Nigerian blockade of Biafran ports and food sources.

Achebe worked tirelessly for the Biafran cause and was nearly killed himself. He traveled to Britain and the United States in a desperate plea for moral and financial aid, but in January 1970, Biafra was finally forced to surrender.

Achebe continued to write and teach in Nigeria and then in 1972 traveled to the United States to take a teaching post at the University of Massachusetts at Amherst. He has since held faculty positions at the University of Connecticut, UCLA, Dartmouth, and the City University of

Disabled veterans of the Biafran civil war in 1967 make their way back to their village outside of Enugu, Nigeria, on March 29, 1998. Kasmir Muba (right) lost his leg to a mine during the conflict. Thirty years after the war, a sense of betrayal and anger was still simmering among the Igbo people.

New York. In 1990, he was seriously injured in an automobile accident in Nigeria that left him paralyzed from the waist down. Professor Leon Botstein, the president of Bard College, approached Achebe during his stay in a London hospital with the offer of a specially endowed chair at the small upstate New York college. Botstein explained, "I went after Chinua Achebe because he is one of the great intellectual and ethical figures of our times. [In his view,] a great deal of the discussion of multiculturalism today is canned. It reduces and essentializes African and black experience. I thought it important for students to hear Achebe, who combines multiculturalism and wisdom."[8] Achebe, who now resides permanently in the United States, has been the recipient of thirty honorary degrees from various American, British, Canadian, and European universities.

Achebe has been highly critical of ongoing Nigerian government corruption in books such as *A Man of the People, Biafran Lunch*, and *The Trouble With Nigeria*. In 2004, he refused an award from the Government of Nigeria as a protest against the anti-Democratic policies of the current government. He and his wife, Christie, a Bard College Education professor, have four children. On November 16, 2000, he celebrated his 70th birthday in a moving public ceremony at Bard College with African-American writer, Toni Morrison.

In the early 1960s, Heinemann, Achebe's publisher, began publishing new African novels in inexpensive paperback editions. Over the past four decades, *Things Fall Apart* has outsold all of the other three hundred African novels combined in the Heinemann catalog.

Today, *Things Fall Apart* continues to be the Great African Novel. What is the secret of its enduring power?

# CHAPTER 2

# Plot

It has been pointed out by critics such as Abdul Janmohamed that of the 118 pages that comprise Part One of *Things Fall Apart*, only eight (or about 7% of the total), strictly speaking, are concerned with plot. There is simply not a lot of plot in *Things Fall Apart*. Why? Because Achebe is far more interested in introducing the reader to the complexities of Igbo culture than in simply advancing a story.

Most of the book is devoted to the depiction of the central events in the life of an agrarian community: planting, harvesting, and the various festivals that accompany them, such as the Feast of the New Yam; the Week of Peace; and more familiar rituals such as marriages and funerals. Only a partial list of Igbo culture and traditions covered in *Things Fall Apart* would include village meetings, Igbo law (the legal spiritual court of the *egwugwu*), family life, community values, patri-archy, marriages, and funerals. The reader also learns about Igbo titles and Igbo religion, with its emphasis on ancestor consciousness as personified by the *egwugwu* and its ceremonies such as the breaking of the Kola, the concept of the *chi*, Igbo gods, and the power wielded by the Oracle. Along the way, we become acquainted with the physical lay-out of an Igbo village, as well as that of the compound of a prosperous man such as Okonkwo.

**PATRIARCHY**
A community in which the father is the head of the family and men have authority over women and children.

The nearest thing to a consecutive story line in Part One is the tale of the unfortunate boy Ikemefuna whom Okonkwo and other men of the village kill when his death is ordered by the Oracle.

# Part One

Part One introduces us to the character of Okonkwo and to village and family life in Igboland (eastern Nigeria) in the 1860s, just before the coming of Christian missionaries and the subsequent British colonization.

Okonkwo is a wealthy and respected warrior of the Umuofia clan. He has prospered by working hard and being as deliberately unlike his lazy, pleasure-loving father as he can be. Okonkwo finds his twelve-year-old son, Nwoye, to be lazy, so he beats and nags the boy constantly. Okonkwo is given custody of a young boy, Ikemefuna, a hostage from a neighboring village with which Okonkwo's village has been at war. Ikemefuna endears himself to Okonkwo and his family and Okonkwo and Ikemefuna come to care for one another as father and son. Actually, Okonkwo's favorite child is his daughter, Ezinma, and he frequently voices regret that Ezinma is not a boy.

Okonkwo beats one of his three wives during the Week of Peace. He is sharply reprimanded by a

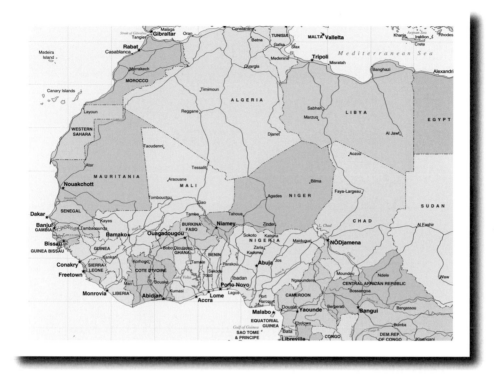

A modern map of Western Africa.

local priest, Ezeani, for his action: "The evil you have done can ruin the whole clan."

Then the Oracle decides that the boy, Ikemefuna, must be killed. Okonkwo is warned by a respected village elder to take no part in the boy's death. But he joins the execution party and even strikes the fatal blow. When Okonkwo returns home from the killing, Nwoye intuits that his friend and surrogate brother is dead. Okonkwo himself sinks into a depression. He feels weak and cannot sleep or eat.

Very early one morning, Okonkwo's second wife, Ekwefi, wakens Okonkwo and tells him that Ezinma is dying. We learn

**ORACLE**
A divinely inspired giver of sacred revelations.

that Ekwefi's nine other children died in infancy. Chileo, in her role as priestess, informs Ekwefi that Agbala, Oracle of the Hills and Caves, wishes to see Ezinma. Chileo takes Ezinma on her back and forbids anyone to follow. Ekwefi follows anyway as does Okonkwo who follows at a distance so that Ezinma is not aware of it. Chileo, carrying Ezinma, makes her rounds of the nine villages. Then with Ezinma still on her back, she enters a cave. Ekwefi waits anxiously outside the cave. Just before dawn, Ekwefi turns and screams when she sees a man in the semi-darkness carrying a machete. It is Okonkwo who has come to protect her and Ezinma. Soon after, Ekwefi and Okonkwo return to the village, and Chileo brings Ezinma back home to Ekwefi's bed and lays the child down to a restoring sleep.

Okonkwo's family prepares for Obierika's daughter's *uri*, or betrothal ceremony, and the feast is a great success. The death of Ezeudu, a village elder, is then announced to the surrounding villages with the *ekwe*, a musical instrument. At his funeral, the men beat drums and fire their guns. Okonkwo's gun accidentally explodes and kills Ezeudu's sixteen-year-old son. Killing a clansman is a crime against the earth goddess, so Okonkwo must atone by taking himself and his family into exile for seven years. According to tribal tradition, the men from Ezeudu's quarter burn Okonkwo's buildings and kill his animals to cleanse the village of his sins.

## Part Two

Part Two is concerned with the period of Okonkwo's exile at Mbanta. It is also during this time that the first Christian missionaries begin to arrive in Umuofia.

Okonkwo's maternal uncle, Uchendu, and the rest of his kinsmen in Mbanta welcome him and help him build a new compound of huts and lend him yam seeds to start a farm. During the second year of Okonkwo's exile, Obierika brings several bags of cowries to Okonkwo. He also brings bad news. A village named Abame has been destroyed by white men.

Two years later, Obierika comes back to Mbanta to visit Okonkwo again. He tells Okonkwo he has seen Nwoye with some of the Christian missionaries who have arrived. Most of the other converts have been *efulefu*, men who hold no status and who are generally ignored by their clan.

When Nwoye returns, Okonkwo chokes him by the neck. Nwoye leaves his father's compound and travels to a Christian school back in Umuofia

The interior of an Igbo home.

to learn reading and writing. The church wins
many converts from the *efulefu*. Okonkwo urges
the men of Mbanta to drive the Christians out with
violence, but the village elders decide to ostracize
them instead. As Okonkwo's seven years of exile
draw to an end, he provides a large feast for his
mother's kinsmen.

## Part Three

In Part Three, Okonkwo returns home to Umuofia and finds that much has changed in his absence. The church has grown in strength and white men subject the villagers to their own British colonial judicial system and rules of government. Sorrowfully, Obierika explains to Okonkwo that the church has weakened the ties of kinship and that it is too late to drive the white men out. Many of the clansmen are now on the white man's side.

Mr. Brown, a white missionary, is a moderate, reasonable man who restrains his flock from antagonizing the clan. He builds a hospital and a school. When Mr. Brown's health begins to fail, Reverend James Smith, a strict and intolerant white man, replaces him. One of his converts, Enoch, dares to unmask an *egwugwu* during an annual ceremony to honor the earth deity, an act equivalent to killing an ancestral spirit. The next day, the *egwugwu* burn Enoch's compound to the ground. Soon after, they confront the Reverend Smith and burn the church as well.

Okonkwo and the rest of the villagers arm themselves with guns and machetes and prepare for a battle. The British district commissioner (or "D.C.") requests that the leaders of Umuofia meet with him. He tricks them, and they are handcuffed and thrown in jail.

After their release, the men return to the village. Okonkwo shows up for a village meeting the next morning wearing traditional battle dress. Five court messengers approach the crowd and tell their leaders to order the meeting to end. Okonkwo suddenly kills one of the messengers with two strokes of his machete. The other villagers allow the other messengers to escape. Okonkwo realizes that the rest of the village is unwilling to go to war against the white men. Okonkwo then goes off alone, now a hunted man.

The district commissioner arrives at Okonkwo's compound and finds a small group of men waiting outside. He threatens to imprison them all if they do not lead him to Okonkwo. Obierika agrees, and they discover Okonkwo's body dangling from a tree behind the compound. He has hanged himself.

Obierika explains that suicide is a grave sin and his clansmen may not touch Okonkwo's body. Obierika lashes out at the D.C., blaming him for Okonkwo's death and praises his friend's greatness. The D.C. orders his Igbo court messengers to do the work of disposing of Okonkwo's body. As he departs the scene, he congratulates himself on adding to his knowledge of local African customs. The book ends with the D.C. working on a book about Africa and imagining that the circumstances of Okonkwo's death would make an interesting paragraph or two. He has already chosen the title: *The Pacification of the Primitive Tribes of the Lower Niger.*

# CHAPTER 3

# Narrative Style

The narrative tone of *Things Fall Apart*, especially in Part One, is to a startling degree, structurally and stylistically much closer to that of an Igbo folktale than to a Western novel.

Achebe's narrative style has been described by critics as paratactic, or consisting of a series of short, simple sentences such as would be naturally used by an oral storyteller recounting the tale to a group of friends and local people sitting around a campfire.

*Parataxis*, from Greek meaning "the act of placing side by side," is a literary technique used in writing or speaking that favors short, simple sentences, often without the use of conjunctions.

This is consistent with the oral African culture Achebe chooses to represent.

Yet, Achebe's book follows the form of a modern Western novel: (1) It is written down and not spoken; (2) It has chapters and a considerable number of pages; (3) It has a theme illustrated by characters and events.

But it is essentially a piece of African, oral storytelling wrapped up in the form of a modern novel and written in English. For that reason, *Things Fall Apart* has been called a syncretic work: a piece of writing that is a synthesis or artful combination of two different elements. In this case, it is a Western novel written in English, but told, for the most part, in the manner of African oral storytelling.

Consider the famous opening paragraph of *Things Fall Apart*:

> *Okonkwo was well known through the nine villages and even beyond. His fame rested on solid personal achievements. As a young man of eighteen he had brought honor*

*to his village by throwing Amalinze the Cat. Amalinze was*
*the great wrestler who for seven years was unbeaten, from*
*Umuofia to Mbaino. He was called the Cat because his*
*back would never touch the earth. It was this man that*
*Okonkwo threw in a fight.*[1]

The paragraph, as Achebe wrote it, is typical of oral expression. It displays a combination of familiar storytelling elements such as:

1. Addition: one fact placed after another.

2. Juxtaposition: one statement placed beside another.

3. Aggregation: a collection of statements that adds up to a whole.

Note the text's absence of coordinating or subordinating conjunctions: *and, that, when, who*. Note also the deliberate *flatness* of the structure. One fact is not presented as any more significantor important than another.

Also, the writer makes no attempt to explain to a modern reader where any of the geographic

An Igbo house, as photographed in the early 1900s.

places or units named ("the nine villages,"
"Umuofia," "Mbaino") actually are or were. He
just assumes, as a local storyteller telling a story to
local people gathered around a campfire would,
that his listeners already know.

In *Things Fall Apart*, as in oral societies,
recurrence or repetition is very important. It is
simply a way of communicating what is most

important or significant. We learn that something is very important not because the author tells us it is so important, ("The most important thing was . . . ") but simply because the author keeps mentioning or repeating the same fact over and over again.

At times virtually identical statements are repeated. Chapter 3 begins: "Okonkwo did not have the start in life which many young men usually had."[2] This is followed by a depiction of his father's laziness, and ends with his father's dishonorable death as he is buried in the Evil Forest. Then, on the following page, Achebe repeats his opening statement: "With a father like Unoka, Okonkwo did not have the start in life which many young people had"[3] and he goes on to tell the reader that despite Okonkwo's starting with nothing because of his lazy father, he had worked "like one possessed" to set himself up for a prosperous future.

He uses the technique in a different way near the end of the book. Achebe writes about Nwoye's having abandoned his native religion to become a Christian, "But there was a young lad who had been captivated (by Christianity). His name was Nwoye, Okonkwo's first son."[4] By now, the reader has already been introduced to Nwoye many pages earlier, at the beginning of the story. Nwoye first appears in the story on page 13: "Okonkwo's first son, Nwoye, was then twelve years old but was already causing his father great anxiety."[5]

It is not that the narrator of the story has forgotten, more than a hundred pages later, who Nwoye is. Rather, it is the process of "remembering," in public, as an oral storyteller would, about the existence of a fact or a character. "Now that boy we told you about earlier . . . Remember, we told you that Okonkwo had a son? Well, now here he is again, that son, and we'll tell you what happened to him." The storyteller might have begun telling his story the day before, and so names and facts that might not have been remembered through a night of sleep, would have to be repeated the next day.

Oral tradition was the norm long before the invention of the printing press made it possible to write things down and store information. Another interesting example of Achebe's oral storytelling technique is that he gives the impression through his use of language, that the story of Okonkwo was already common knowledge among the Igbo people, ("Okonkwo was well known throughout the nine villages and even beyond") and his tale was already a well known popular "myth." This was not true, but it successfully sets a "heroic" or "mythic" tone that he carries through to the end of the story.

The Jesuit scholar Walter Ong maintained that there were three characteristics of oral or storytelling cultures: (1) Communication usually takes place in a community setting. (2) People talk to one another; (3) Communication is usually *external*. It often takes place in a group setting, in a big community meeting, or with one neighbor talking to another.[6]

In a modern western novel, or in a

Shakespeare play, a character will often talk or think to himself aloud in a speech called a soliloquy. Communication is more *internal*. In Shakespeare's most famous soliloquy, Hamlet talks to himself while he contemplates suicide:

*To be, or not to be; that is the question:*
*Whether 'tis nobler in the mind to suffer*
*The slings and arrows of outrageous fortune,*
*Or to take arms against a sea of troubles,*
*And by opposing end them?*[7]

In many modern novels, the author takes the reader inside the characters' heads and we learn what they are thinking internally. We learn about their inner desires and conflicts. Here is a passage from Dostoyevsky's *Crime and Punishment*. The young Russian student, Raskolnikov, has committed

*Hamlet* is a play written by William Shakespeare circa 1600 in which the title character returns home from abroad to discover his father has died and that his uncle (his father's brother) has married his mother. After learning that his uncle is responsible for murdering his father, Hamlet struggles over whether or not he should take revenge.

Fyodor Dostoevsky (1821–1881) is considered one of the great figures of Russian literature and one of the most influential writers of the last two centuries. His novels often feature characters living in terrible poverty and experiencing extreme states of mind. They deal with the human psyche while also analysing the political, social, and spiritual states of the Russia of his time.

a murder and fears he is being tricked by the police into confessing:

> *Raskolnikov walked straight home. He was so muddled and bewildered that on getting home he sat for a quarter of an hour on the sofa, trying to collect his thoughts. He did not attempt to think about Nikolay; he was stupified; he felt that his confession was something inexplicable, amazing— something beyond his understanding.*[8]

Raskolnikov and many modern characters are isolated. They sit in their own little apartments and furnished rooms and examine and reexamine their own lives, actions, and thoughts. They live largely inside their own heads. But in a piece of oral writing such as *Things Fall Apart*, we learn about the various characters by seeing them in action and interaction.

Here is another technique Achebe employs, one that is more common in oral storytelling. He tells the reader what a character is thinking and feeling but he uses concrete objects to tell us. Near the end of *Things Fall Apart*, Okonkwo is sitting alone by a fire thinking about Nwoye and how disappointed he is in his son. Achebe might have written the scene like this:

> *He sighed heavily as he sat by the fire and thought about his son. Suddenly he had a deep insight and he saw things as they really were. It was clear that he, Okonkwo, who was a real and powerfully alive man had produced a weak-spirited son who was really no man at all.*

Achebe chose to write the scene differently. He used a concrete object, the dying fire, to personify the relationship between Okonkwo and his son:

> *He sighed heavily, and as if in sympathy the smoldering log also sighed. And immediately Okonkwo's eyes were opened*

*and he saw the whole matter clearly. Living fire begets cold, impotent ash. He sighed again, deeply.*[9]

Ong stressed that in oral, non-literate societies, the lack of writing (and reading) makes it more difficult to think or communicate in intellectual or abstract ways. This is because very little thought can be kept or maintained the way we store and maintain important facts today in computers or in books. That is why non-literate, oral societies fall back on using proverbs, which, like simple songs and catchy slogans, are easy to remember.

Ong makes this point very strongly with regard to the great, Greek poet Homer. Homer composed the great, Greek epics, *The Iliad* and *The Odyssey*. These epic poems were originally not written but spoken, and passed on from one

*The Iliad* and *The Odyssey* are two ancient, epic poems composed by the legendary Greek writer, Homer. *The Iliad* centers around the Greek soldier Achilles as the Greeks battle with Troy in the conflict known as the Trojan War. *The Odyssey* deals with the ten-year effort of Odysseus to return home to Greece after the Trojan War has ended.

storyteller to another. Each storyteller had the task of remembering the story and retelling it.

Ong notes that "Homeric Greeks valued cliches (or proverbs) because . . . the poets . . . relied upon the formulaic constitution of thought."[10] It was simply a very reliable way to remember great amounts of spoken material.

# CHAPTER 4

# Themes

The theme of *Things Fall Apart* is best stated by
Achebe himself:

> *This theme—put quite simply—is that African people did*
> *not hear of culture for the first time from Europeans; that*
> *their societies were not mindless but frequently had a phi-*
> *losophy of great depth and value and beauty, that they had*
> *poetry and, above all, they had dignity. It is this dignity*
> *that many African people all but lost during the colonial*
> *period and it is this that they must now regain.*[1]

This was Achebe's purpose in writing *Things
Fall Apart*—to show his readers the civilized and

complex Igbo society that was supplanted by the British colonialist system.

Three institutions held the Igbo society together. All three are very much a part of the fabric of *Things Fall Apart*: the traditional Igbo religion, which pervaded all aspects of the citizens' lives; their social philosophy known as communitarianism, in which the community was more important than any individual or group of individuals; and their extended family system, which offered a social and economic safety net to anyone in time of need or trouble.

## Religion

*Things Fall Apart* is packed with what Simon Gikandi describes as "countless semiotic codes."[2] Semiotics has been defined as a science which studies the role of signs as part of social life.

Early on in *Things Fall Apart*, Achebe presents a scene in which Okoye visits Unoka, Okonkwo's father, an occasion that begins with the ritual of the breaking of the kola nut:

*Unoka went into an inner room and soon returned with a
small wooden disc containing a kola nut, some alligator
pepper and a lump of white chalk.*

*"I have kola," he announced when he sat down, and
passed the disc over to his guest.*

*"Thank you. He who brings kola brings life. But I think
you ought to break it," replied Okoye, passing back
the disc.*

*"No, it is for you, I think," and they argued like this for a
few moments before Unoka accepted the honor of breaking
the kola. Okoye, meanwhile, took the lump of chalk, drew
some lines on the floor, and then painted his big toe.*

*As he broke the kola, Unoka prayed to their ancestors for
life and health, and for protection against their enemies.*[3]

The kola is a small nut which signifies
friendship and neighborly disposition among the
Igbo. A traditional Igbo man's day or a traditional
public ceremony begins with ritual incantations or
prayers in which the male head of the family
invites and acknowledges the presence of the

dead-living ancestors with three ritual items, *oji* (kola nut), *nzu* (white chalk), and *mmanya ngwuo* (palm wine).

With the wine, he pours a libation on the floor or ground. This symbolically opens the earth so that the ancestors can enter the physical world from the underground world of the spirits. With the chalk, he draws lines on the floor to pray for and symbolize the safe cyclic passage of the ancestors to and from the spirit underground.

**SYMBOL**
Something that stands for, represents or suggests another thing.

The white chalk painted on the big toe is also a sign that signifies the safe arrival of the guest and a prayer for his safe departure. The kola nut is broken and shared among the living, visible men, and the invisible, non-living (the dead), a sign of the spiritual communion and unity intended to bring life and prosperity to the people. The ritual must also precede all traditional Igbo public events, including weddings, naming ceremonies, meetings, and political gatherings. In English-speaking countries, such as the United States and Britain, which have large Igbo communities, the ritual is still conducted between males only, and only in the Igbo language. The reason for this is that the dead-living ancestors, whose presence and attendance are being invoked, do not understand or speak English.

The Igbo, because they are a very religious people, do not separate their religious lives from their secular lives. The religion the Igbo still practice is organized around four theological concepts: (1) Chukwu, the great or "high god," the creator of everything who lives above; (2) non-human spirits, deities, or oracles, and man-made goddesses and oracles, as well as nature gods and goddesses; (3) the dead-living ancestors from whom all Igbo people are reincarnated; and (4) the *chi*. Chi has rough equivalents in other cultures—soul, karma, guardian angel, fate. Kalu Ogbaa describes *chi* as Achebe uses it in *Things Fall Apart* as "variously, a personal god or spirit, guardian angel, soul, or spirit double. Defined by its roles in a man's life, *chi* is creator, fate, or destiny."[4]

## Community/Balance

At the heart of the Igbo view is the enormous importance the Igbo place on *balance*, a notion that pervades every aspect of Igbo society. When Okonkwo violates the Week of Peace by beating his wife, the act is regarded by his shocked neighbors not just as the breaking of a rule but as an extraordinary action.

During other weeks of the year, a man might work excessively hard and even quarrel with his neighbors and family. But not during the Week of Peace, when the Igbo sense of balance required that everyone, without exception, suspend all work and avoid the slightest quarrel or aggressive act. To do otherwise was a grievous insult to the earth goddess.

Anthonia C. Kalu writes about the Igbo emphasis on balance as it is applied to the roles of men and women in Igbo society:

*On the surface, Igbo society seems predominantly patriarchal;*
*however, women wield a considerable amount of influence.*
*The idea of woman as counterpart to man is strongly*
*emphasized. The female principle is revered. In the Igbo*
*pantheon, the most revered and feared deity is Ana, the*
*Earth Goddess . . . In Things Fall Apart, Achebe portrays*
*how the Week of Peace is held to 'honor our great goddess*
*of the earth without whose blessings our crops will not grow.*[5]

## Community

The Igbo regard for balance and moderation is at
the heart of Igbo communal affairs, and any viola-
tion of it is a threat to the whole community.
Achebe takes pains to make a distinction between
the Umuofia of *Things Fall Apart,* which is obviously patriarchal, and the larger Igbo society
and culture. Igbo society places enormous importance on balance between the genders, through
the equal weight it places on gods and goddesses,
priests and priestesses as well as the feminine
and masculine principles.

The Igbo worldview allows for the simultaneous functioning of many different and sometimes antagonistic elements. People are counseled to thread their way carefully so as to avoid offending any of the contending spirits. Extremism of any kind is discouraged and considered dangerous. This same healthy respect and regard for balance and moderation is the norm in Igbo communal affairs. No Igbo community will make war on its neighbors without carefully considering reasonable alternatives first.

*Things Fall Apart* begins with an emergency town meeting and there are a number of other such town meetings scattered throughout the book. The gathering in the village square is attended by as many as 10,000 men of Umuofia. They have assembled to discuss the question of how to respond to the murder of an Umuofian woman by a man from a neighboring village. Should the village declare war? "Many others spoke, and at the end it was decided to follow the normal course of action,"[6] which, in this instance, turns out to be a wise and moderate one. "Umuofia . . . never went to war unless its case was clear and just."[7]

Later in *Things Fall Apart*, it is the very gift for balance and moderation that keeps the Umuofians from behaving so foolishly as to engage in a suicidal war with their British military occupiers. However, Achebe does not romanticize or idealize the Igbo society he portrays. It is obviously far from perfect as the same Oracle of the Hills and Caves who wisely keeps Umuofia from going to war is the same deity who later decides that Ikemefuna must be killed, a decision that seems utterly wrong and senseless. Another disturbing aspect of Igbo religion is the belief that the birth of twins is an evil event. The unfortunate babies must not be permitted to live but be left out in the Evil Forest to die.

## Extended Family System

The Igbo extended family system is best illustrated by the welcome assistance Okonkwo receives from his Uncle Uchendu of his mother's side of the family when he loses his home and other property and is forced into exile in the neighboring village of Mbanta.

In another society, such as our own, an individual might be ruined by such a calamity and be forced to start over from scratch. But not in the Igbo society of *Things Fall Apart,* in which close ties of mutual support were maintained with both the male (or paternal) and female (or maternal) branches of a family. An Igbo woman, for example, cannot marry a man from her own village but is required by Igbo law to marry a man from a neighboring village. It is a thoughtfully balanced system that offers a wide safety net and a strong stabilizing influence that helps to hold the society together and keep it strong.

As a result, Okonkwo is given a new compound in which he and his wives and children may live. Uchendu also provides him with enough seed-yams to plant a sizable crop with which to feed his family and send the surplus to market.

**A tribal meeting of Igbo elders**

## Poetry

There is often a timeless and poetic quality
about the lost world Achebe is describing in
*Things Fall Apart*:

> It seemed to Ekwefi that the night had become a little
> lighter. The cloud had lifted and a few stars were out. The

*moon must be preparing to rise, its sullenness over. When*
*the moon rose late in the night, people said it was refusing*
*food, as a sullen husband refuses his wife's food when they*
*have quarreled.* [8]

It is a world, a culture, a way of life that existed undisturbed for hundreds if not thousands of years. There is also the lead up to the public wrestling match in the center of the village playground:

*The wrestlers were not there yet and the drummers held the*
*field . . . Behind them was the big and ancient silk–cotton*
*tree which was sacred. Spirits of good children lived in that*
*tree waiting to be born. On ordinary days young women*
*who desired children came to sit under its shade.* [9]

If Achebe were a visual artist instead of a writer, *Things Fall Apart* would be a rich and highly detailed tapestry depicting a multitude of customs, institutions, and traditions of Igbo life as they existed before the coming of colonial rule. And what would be at its center? Balance. Duality. Respect for the individual. Respect for the values of the community.

In a word: dignity.

# CHAPTER 5

# Literary Devices

The question has often been asked: If Achebe were so determined to write a purely "African" novel, why did he not write in Igbo instead of English?

Kalu Ogbaa writes:

> Achebe's peculiar use of the English language, as he plays the role of novelist as teacher, makes him a spokesman for his people, but he does not 'speak to the colonized people only.' He also speaks to the colonizers and to their spectators of the colonial conflicts between the Igbo and the white men, particularly spectators in Europe and America where his novels are read.[1]

But Achebe still wanted a novel that was essentially African, and he infused as many Igbo and African elements into its writing as he could manage. R. Angogo says, "In his books . . . Achebe uses a language I would like to refer to as 'Ibo in English.'"[2]

A prime example of this "Ibo in English" is the scene in which Ekwefi, Okonkwo's second wife, is preparing dinner in her hut in Okonkwo's compound when she hears a voice call out her name:

> *"Ekwefi!" a voice called from one of the other huts. It was Nwoye's mother, Okonkwo's first wife.*
> *"Is that me?" Ekwefi called back.*[3]

A writer attempting to put the question into English would have had Ekwefi answer "Is that me you're calling?" But that was not the way an Igbo of that time would have answered. Why? Because of the Igbo belief that an evil spirit calls human beings once and that if they answered "yes," they would die. "That was the way people answered calls from the outside. They never answered yes for fear it might be an evil spirit calling."[4]

Kalu Ogbaa cites other examples of exact Igbo phrasings in *Things Fall Apart* such as when Ekwefi tells Chielo how upset she was by Okonkwo's firing his gun at her: "I cannot yet find a mouth with which to tell the story."[5]

Chielo, who is also a priestess, responds, "Your *chi* is very much awake, my friend," speaking more in her theological role as if to credit Ekwefi's escape from harm to her guardian angel or spirit-double.[6]

Simon Gikandi notes that just as Achebe fills *Things Fall Apart* with semiotic codes and the incidents of everyday life in the Igboland of the late nineteenth century, he uses literary and linguistic devices in a continuing pursuit of a deep verbal texture of "Africanness."[7] There are many examples of figurative language: proverbs, didactic

**DIDACTIC**
That which is intended to teach a moral point or lesson.

animal tales (i.e., "the little bird *nza*") involving animal imagery, as well as folk songs, chants, and exotic imagery used by priests, diviners, and titled men as well as the ordinary language of everyday people peculiar to that part of Africa.

A primary Igbo mode of expression was the proverb. Indeed Kalu Ogbaa says that "proverbs are among the easily distinguishable folkways in Achebe's novels."[8]

## Proverbs

Achebe practically starts out *Things Fall Apart* with a discourse on proverbs and their importance to the Igbo.

Okoye, a wealthy and successful man, comes to visit Okonkwo's shiftless father, Unoka, who owes money all over the village. Okoye is clearly leading up to asking Unoka for the money he owes him. But he does not, at least not right away: "Having spoken plainly so far, Okoye said the next half dozen sentences in proverbs. Among the Ibo the art of conversation is regarded very highly, and proverbs are the palm-oil with which words are eaten."[9]

Kalu Ogbaa notes: "The metaphor is significant because there is hardly any Igbo menus or recipe that does not include palm oil, just as there is hardly any good Igbo speech without the speaker interlacing it with some proverbs."[10]

Like any smooth and liquid vegetable oil, when an Igbo cooks with it or mixes it in with food, it makes the food easier to eat and digest. In the same way, familiar proverbs, often commonly used witty sayings, are used to make conversations flow more smoothly and make difficult statements or sentiments easier to accept or digest.

What exactly is a proverb? A witty or clever saying often handed down from generation to generation that reveals an easily understandable truth. Proverbs, because they are easily remembered, do not have to be written down and are a medium of expression favored by non-literate peoples. Time-honored proverbs such as "A rolling stone gathers no moss," "A penny saved is a penny earned," and "Never judge a book by its cover" are very common in our own culture.

Proverbs are by their very nature didactic (designed to teach) and reflective of the values of the society in which they are used. "Achebe is a didactic writer," notes Richard K. Priebe, a statement with which Achebe himself would readily concur. Priebe goes on to note that the proverbs that Achebe employs "are important elements in the whole system of values that *Things Fall Apart* reflects, elements as it were of a very large proverb."[11]

Virtually all the proverbs in *Things Fall Apart* support the prevailing Igbo notions of balance, flexibility, and acceptance of other people's customs and preferences. For example: "Never make an early morning appointment with a man who has just married a new wife," and "Where one thing stands, another stands beside it."

Kalu Ogbaa sees three different types of proverbs in *Things Fall Apart:*

*Commendatory proverbs, such as praise hard work and achievement. The narrator, speaking for the elders, praises Okonkwo: "As the elders said, if a child washed his hands he could eat with kings. Okonkwo had clearly washed his hands and so he ate with kings and elders."*[12]

> *If ever a man deserved his success, that man was Okonkwo. At an early age he had achieved fame as the greatest wrestler in all the land. That was not luck. At the most one could say that his chi or personal god was good. But the Ibo people have a proverb that when a man says yes his chi says yes also. Okonkwo said yes very strongly; so his chi agreed.*[13]

Ogbaa also refers to admonitory proverbs, which are intended to be critical of the persons to whom they are addressed. At a village meeting, Okonkwo insults another man who is not as successful as himself. An elder immediately puts Okonkwo in his place: "The oldest man present said sternly that those whose palm kernels were cracked for them by a benevolent spirit should not forget to be humble."[14] Okonkwo apologizes for his insulting remark and the meeting continues.

## Animal Tales/Folk Stories

In our own culture, there are examples of teaching animal stories such as "The Tortoise and the Hare." In this story, the victory of the slow but purposeful tortoise shows the triumph of quiet determination and persistence over sheer speed and talent. In Igbo culture, animal tales that teach a lesson are also highly popular.

If there is one "very large proverb" in *Things Fall Apart*, it is the story of the little bird Nza which practically foretells the whole tale of Okonkwo's rise and fall in a few simple sentences:

> And as people said he [Okonkwo] had no respect for the gods of the clan. His enemies said his good fortune had gone to his head. They called him the little bird Nza who so far forgot himself after a heavy meal that he challenged his chi.[15]

Like the little bird Nza who becomes too heavy to fly after eating a heavy meal, Okonkwo makes the mistake of becoming too full of himself and his own wealth and power.

Another animal tale is that of the tortoise who tries to trick the birds and ends up crashing to the earth and breaking his shell in pieces instead. The moral of the story is best summed up by Tortoise's own comment, "I have learned that a man who makes trouble for others is also making it for himself."[16]

The story of the Mosquito and Ear appears as Okonkwo is beginning to get over his depression after the murder of Ikemefuna. Its placement at this point in the story is significant.

> He [Okonkwo] began to wonder why he had felt uneasy at all. . . . He stretched himself and scratched his thigh where a mosquito had bitten him as he had slept . . . Why do they always go for one's ears? When he was a child his mother had told him a story about it. But it was as silly as all women's stories. Mosquito, she said, had asked Ear to

*marry him, whereupon Ear fell on the floor in uncontrol-*

*lable laughter. "How much longer do you think you will*

*live?" she asked. "You are already a skeleton." Mosquito*

*went away humiliated, and any time he passed her way*

*he told Ear that he was still alive.*[17]

The word "skeleton" is significant here. Mosquito could be seen as Okonkwo's conscience and Ear as Okonkwo's own psyche, his subconscious, still guilty over the murder of Ikemefuna. In his refusal to face the reality of what he has done, he laughs at Mosquito. But Mosquito is still buzzing around and bothers him greatly. The story ends with "any time he passed her way he told Ear he was still alive."

The message is clear. The memory of Ikemefuna will not go away and will continue to haunt Okonkwo.

# Imagery and Symbolism

Achebe's novels are full of Igbo similes and
metaphors, and figures of speech that characterize
the speech patterns of his Igbo characters:

> He [Nwoye] even remembered how he had laughed when
> Ikemefuna told him that the proper name for a corn cob
> with only a few scattered grains was eze-agadi-nwayi, or
> the teeth of an old woman.[18]

There is also a recurrent use of wrestling
imagery. Okonkwo wrestles with his two selves; his
softer inner side and his more aggressive outward
self. In essence he wrestles with his own *chi*. Later
he wrestles with his own kinsmen about how to
deal with the power of the British newcomers.

Another piece of prominent imagery involves
the coming of the locusts which portend the series
of natural and man-made disasters that descend
on Umuofia and Okonkwo's life: the coming of
the white man, the drought that destroys his
crops, his exile after the accidental killing of
Ezeudu's son, and his own eventual suicide.

# Religious Terminology and Allusions

When Achebe describes Okonkwo's fears of failure he uses words such as Igbo men use in describing the forces of evil before the white missionaries came:

> But his whole life was dominated by fear, the fear of failure and of weakness. It was deeper and more intimate than the fear of evil and capricious gods and of magic, the fear of the forest, and of the forces of nature, malevolent, red in tooth and claw.[19]

# Folk Songs and Chants

Folk songs and chants in *Things Fall Apart* call up what Ogbaa calls "a wealth of associations that informs his readers about Igbo mores and values. There are songs of praise which express people's admiration for achievers such as celebrated public wrestlers.

> Who will wrestle for our village?
> Okafo will wrestle for our village.
> Has he thrown a hundred men?

Igbo musicians playing traditional Igbo instruments.

*He has thrown four hundred men."* [20]

Homiletic songs teach or persuade. Thus Okonkwo's uncle, Uchendu, counsels him to stop feeling sorry for himself because he has been sent into exile. The old man then tells Okonkwo about all the misfortunes he has survived: five dead wives, twenty-two buried children, and concludes: "Have you not heard the song they sing when a woman dies?"

> *'For whom is it well, for whom is it well?*
> *There is no one for whom it is well.'* [21]

## Bridal Songs

The musicians at the wedding of Obierika's daughter sing a popular bridal song:

> *If I hold her hand*
> *She says, 'Don't touch!'*
> *If I hold her foot*
> *She says, 'Don't touch!'*
> *But when I hold her waist–beads*
> *She pretends not to know.* [22]

The song reveals much about sexual mores among the Igbo. A young woman's virginity is highly cherished and every Igbo bride is expected to be a virgin. The penalty for premarital sex by a bride is severe, ranging from public disgrace to annulment of the marriage contract.

## Work Songs

Work songs are, of course, meant to be sung as people work.

> *Kotma of the ash buttocks,*
> *He is fit to be a slave.*
> *The white man has no sense,*
> *He is fit to be a slave.*[23]

This is sung by angry Igbo men who have been locked up by the British and supervised by corrupt court messengers. *Kotma* was the name the Igbo gave to the hated Igbo court messengers whose "ash buttocks" referred to the ash or white-colored shorts they wore.

## Play Songs

There are also play songs:

> *The rain fell in thin, slanting showers through sunshine*
>
> *and quiet breeze. Children no*
>
> *longer stayed indoors but ran about singing:*
>
> *'The rain is falling, the sun is shining,*
>
> *Alone Nnadi is cooking and eating.'* [24]

The most poignant and ironic song in *Things Fall Apart* is the song sung by Ikemefuna as, unknowingly, he walks to his death. He thinks about his mother whom he has not seen in three years.

> *His mother might be dead. He tried in vain to force the*
>
> *thought out of his mind. Then he tried to settle the matter*
>
> *the way he used to settle such matters when he was a little*
>
> *boy. He still remembered the song.*
>
> *Eze elina, elina!*

**irony**—The incongruity of an expected situation (or its outcome) and the actual situation (or its outcome). In language, irony is the deliberate use of words to contrast an apparent meaning with the words' intended meaning (which are usually the complete opposite of each other).

*Eze ilikwa ya*

*Ikwaba akwa oligholi*

*Ebe Danda nechi eze*

*Ebe Uzuzu nete egwu*

*Sala*

*He sang it in his mind, and walked to its beat. If the song ended on his right foot, his mother was alive. If it ended on his left, she was dead.*[25]

A few more steps and his own life ends.

# CHAPTER 6

# Major Characters

There is really only one major character in *Things Fall Apart*. The character of Okonkwo dominates *Things Fall Apart* to such an extent that a German edition of the novel was titled simply "Okonkwo." Achebe introduces Okonkwo as a larger than life seemingly mythological character "tall and huge, and his bushy eyebrows and wide nose gave him a severe look . . . When he walked, his heels hardly touched the ground and he seemed to walk on springs, as if he was going to pounce on some-body."[1]

Okonkwo is more than just an intimidating figure. "He did pounce on people quite often . . . He had no patience with unsuccessful men. He had had no patience with his father."[2]

We are told absolutely nothing of Okonkwo's mother, but we quickly learn that his father was "lazy and . . . quite incapable of thinking about tomorrow."[3] Although some critics see Okonkwo as representative of traditional Igbo society, Neil Ten Kortenaar points out that there is one important "detail that does not fit with Okonkwo's representative status and that makes him an individual in time, and that is his relationship with his father."[4]

When he was a child, Okonkwo was mortified to hear a friend call his father an *agbala*. Although he knew the term *agbala* was often used as another name for a woman, he learned it also refers to a man who has taken no title. The shame Okonkwo felt over this was reinforced when his father, Unoka, died of an affliction considered so abominable to the goddess that he was not even allowed a burial.

Deprived of an inheritance that could have provided him a reference for who he was or what he might become, Okonkwo is determined to become as unlike his father as possible. Where Unoka hated war and the sight of blood, Okonkwo becomes known far and wide as a fierce wrestler and warrior with a collection of five heads. Whereas Unoka was always lazy and in debt, Okonkwo works hard to build up his wealth, eventually acquiring three wives and "barnsfull of yam."

We are told Okonkwo had a stammer and we might surmise that it developed in reaction to his father's ease with language and love of storytelling. Yet, as Solomon O. Iyasere notes, "In violently repudiating all that his father represented, Okonkwo repudiates not only his undignified irresponsibility, but also those positive qualities of love and compassion and sensitivity."[5] These he considers feminine and instinctively represses in fear of appearing weak: "Perhaps down in his heart Okonkwo was not a cruel man. But his whole life was dominated by fear, the fear of failure and of weakness. . . . It was not external but lay deep within himself. It was the fear of himself, lest he should be found to resemble his father."[6]

Okonkwo's difficult relationship with his father is duplicated in his relationship with his own eldest son, Nwoye. The boy's gentle nature is troubling to Okonkwo, who thinks his son unmanly. The idea that Nwoye might be the reincarnation of the very man whose memory Okonkwo is determined to wipe out is too unnerving to consider. Instead, he says, "There is too much of his mother in him" and is determined to beat the softness out of the boy. The sins of the father are thus passed on as young Nwoye develops a fear of his father and eventually rejects him, thus repeating the pattern set by his father.

Though a patriarchic community, the Igbo hold the feminine principle in high regard. For the community to work, each member must balance the male and female principles within himself. Okonkwo, however, cannot do this. Where his father failed because he could not integrate the masculine, Okonkwo fails because he is unable to assimilate the feminine side of his nature.

As Okonkwo represses his softer, "feminine" emotions, a growing resentment smolders and eats away at him, occasionally erupting in passive-aggressive behavior. He does not hesitate, for example, to deal rudely with less successful men. "Okonkwo knew how to kill a man's spirit."[7]

All this is not to say that Okonkwo does not have some softer, more flexible qualities. His affection for Ekwefi, his second wife, Ezinma, his daughter by her, and Ikemefuna are genuine, but to reveal his feelings publicly would, in his eyes, be a weakness and identify him with his father. This he cannot do:

> Okonkwo never showed any emotion openly, unless it be the emotion of anger. To show affection was a sign of weakness; the only thing worth demonstrating was strength. He therefore treated Ikemefuna as he treated everybody else—with a heavy hand.[8]

The decision that Ikemefuna must be killed is not Okonkwo's. Okonkwo has no enthusiasm for killing Ikemefuna, and Ezeudo, the oldest man in the community, explicity warns him against taking part in the boy's death.

But Okonkwo defies Ezeudo's command and goes along with the other men who pretend to escort Ikemefuna on the journey back to his native village, an excursion that will provide the opportunity for his execution. Okonkwo stays to the rear of the procession because his heart is not in the killing. But why does he go along at all? He is afraid of seeming to the others to be soft and weak.

Okonkwo does not strike the first blow, but when Ikemefuna falls and cries out to him, "My father, they have killed me!" what does Okonkwo do? "Dazed with fear, Okonkwo drew his machete and cut him down." Achebe immediately adds, "He was afraid of being thought weak."[9]

When, in an attempt to ease his depression over the slaying, he goes to see his friend Obierika, he says nothing about the killing but only complains to Obierika about Nwoye's lack of manly qualities. It is then that Okonkwo utters what may be the book's cruelest and saddest line when he says to Obierika: "I cannot understand why you refused to come with us to kill that boy."[10] He refuses to give Ikemefuna who came to regard him as a father, the respect of even having had a name. It is as though Okonkwo wants to blot out any memory of him, as though Ikemefuna never existed.

Ironically, it is an accidental shooting that forces him into exile. According to the narrator, "the crime in Igbo society could have been of two kinds, male or female. Okonkwo had committed the female, because it had been inadvertent. He could return to the clan after seven years."[11] The feminine, which he has denied for so long, takes everything away from him. In the ritual cleansing of the land, all of his property is destroyed. The goddess herself sends him into exile, and where does he go but to Mbanta, his mother's land? It seems the more he struggles with the feminine, the more tangled up in it he gets.

Wholly identified with his material world, he is nothing without his house, barns, and yams. Out of touch with his usual external resources, he becomes depressed. Uchendo, his uncle, sees his unhappiness and asks, "why is it that one of the commonest names we give our children is Nneka, or 'Mother is Supreme'? . . . Why is it that when a woman dies she is taken home to be buried with her own kinsmen?"[12]

Okonkwo is thus being offered an important opportunity by his uncle to explore the feminine and develop psychologically, but he does not take it. Not only does he not know the answer, he is not even interested in exploring the question. Clement Okafor concludes "Okonkwo's psyche is so traumatized by his father's penury and the poverty of his early childhood that his psyche remains mortally wounded throughout his life."[13]

At the end of seven years, Okonkwo, grown prosperous again, is eager to resume his position of leadership in Umuofia. Basically unchanged, he returns to a dramatically changed Umuofia.

Not only have Christian missionaries set up a church, but other white men have followed them and set up a government.

Okonkwo's personal story is thus to some extent a microcosm of the larger story of the clan. As Okonkwo's personal world falls apart, so too does the life of the clan. "The clan had undergone such profound change during his exile that it was barely recognizable . . . Okonkwo was deeply grieved. And it was not just a personal grief. He mourned for the clan, which he saw breaking up and falling apart, and he mourned for the warlike men of Umuofia, who had so unaccountably become soft like women."[14]

When Okonkwo first hears of the missionaries, he wants to drive them out by force. As Solomon Iyasere reiterates, "Okonkwo turns to the only means he knows—violence—to solve the problem."[15] The clan at first considers the strangers harmless. But when Nwoye turns to Christianity, Okonkwo " . . . felt a strong desire to take up his machete, go to the church and wipe out the entire vile and miscreant gang."[16] But it is the sudden prospect of his own genealogical termination that stops this man of action and prompts him to ponder why he is "cursed with such a son . . . his son's crime stood out in its stark enormity. . . Suppose when he died all his male children decided to follow Nwoye's steps and abandon their ancestors? Okonkwo felt a cold shudder run through him at the terrible prospect, like the prospect of annihilation."[17]

It is interesting to note that Okonkwo avoids reflecting on the fact that he abandoned his own father. That he could not control his eldest son upset him so much that, finally, gathering his other sons together, he disowns Nwoye.

For a brief moment toward the end, the warrior rises within him. He implores the men of the village to "do something substantial," and the egwugwu respond by burning down the church. Okonkwo begins to feel like his old self again. Soon after, he and the others are arrested and humiliated, Then, after the village pays a fine of

250 cowries, they are finally freed to go home where, undaunted, Okonkwo pulls out his old war dress. "If Umuofia decided on war," he thinks, "all would be well. But if they chose to be cowards he would go out and avenge himself."[18]

But the clan had changed. One might say it had no choice but to submit in the face of a superior military force, and as Solomon O. Iyasere comments, it is "a society that in its flexibility has allowed a place for the white Christian missionaries." It was Okonkwo who would not change. He would not be cowed. Iyasere goes on to say that "like the recalcitrant Rev. Smith, Okonkwo views the situation in terms of absolute, irreconcilable antipodes."[19] Submission to him meant death, and he saw no choice but to fight. When Okonkwo kills the messenger and hears voices ask, "Why did he do it?" He suddenly realizes the clan is not behind him. We feel his terrible isolation and remember his father's words, "It is more difficult and more bitter when a man fails *alone*."[20]

Ironically, Okonkwo's death, like his father's,

is considered an abomination, a sin against the goddess. Despite that and the fact that he does not have a proper burial, Okonkwo remains a great man in his own way, for he was true to himself. He was a warrior ready to fight for his clan, ready to uphold its values, and ready to make one last stand against the enemy. In his passionate lament to the district commissioner, Obierika says, "that man was one of the greatest men in Umuofia."[21]

Physically powerful, ambitious, proud, brave, courageous, and hardworking, Okonkwo seems a mythic figure. Yet his unbridled fear of being anything like his father makes him all too human and drives him to a tragic end. His tragedy, as Iyasere sums up so well, is that "unable to change himself, he [Okonkwo] will not accept change in others, in the world around him, in the people of Umuofia."[22]

# CHAPTER 7

# Minor Characters

## Unoka

Although he dies perhaps years before *Things Fall Apart* begins, Unoka, Okonkwo's father, plays a dominant role. It is fair to say that Unoka exerts a far greater influence in death than he ever did in life. As Simon Gikandi notes, Okonkwo's claim that he is "a self-made man is an illusion," for he "can only define himself against the negative forces represented by his dead father."[1]

Unoka is a fun-loving ne'er do well, a dreamer who loved music, dance, and storytelling. When he played his flute "his face [beamed] with blessedness and peace."[2] He had a great love of beauty and managed to avoid any hard work. In the rare event of money coming into his hands, he spent it immediately on palm wine and friends rather than on his family that often went hungry.

There is not a lot of humor in *Things Fall Apart*. This is perhaps because Okonkwo, who dominates the book, has little sense of balance or perspective and fails to appreciate the humor in his own life or his father. Achebe makes up for this somewhat with a couple of funny stories about Unoka. In one, Unoka complains to the Oracle that he maintains all the correct religious observances such as sacrificing a cock to Ani but still remains in poverty. The Oracle cuts him off almost immediately and reproaches him saying,

> *when a man is at peace with his gods and his ancestors,*
> *his harvest will be good or bad according to the strength*
> *of his arm. You, Unoka, are known in all the clan for*
> *the weakness of your machete and your hoe. . . .*
> *Go home and work like a man.*[3]

In another story, a successful man, Okoye, goes to visit Unoka to ask him to repay some money he owes him. Unoka's reaction is to laugh "loud and long and his voice rang out clear as the *ogene*, and tears stood in his eyes."[4]

The answer is to show his creditor lines of chalk on the far wall of his hut, more than fifty, each representing a debt. Unoka happily explains to Okoye that, of course, he cannot possibly repay him until he repays the much greater sums he owes to other men in the village. "I shall pay my big debts first."[5] Okonkwo, as a child or a man, sees nothing funny or endearing about his father's irresponsible behavior.

## Nwoye

Okonkwo's son Nwoye is as unlike Okonkwo as Okonkwo is unlike Unoka. That Nwoye reminds Okonkwo of his father, whose very memory he seeks to erase, infuriates Okonkwo who determines to beat any softness out of the boy. Like his grandfather, Nwoye takes no interest in war. He seeks beauty and harmony in his world.

Nwoye's values are determined by something within, whereas the material, outer world, determines Okonkwo's values.

So the father/son motif is repeated, but differently. Though Nwoye fears his father, he does not repress his feelings. He questions his father's brutality. He asks other questions as well. For example: Why does the clan leave twin babies to die in the Evil Forest? The brutal sacrificial murder of Ikemefuna likewise horrifies Nwoye.

**MOTIF**
A central idea or theme in a literary work.

Nwoye turns away from both his father and his community. Like other outcasts or *efulefu*, he is drawn to the new religion whose storytelling and poetry speak to something deep inside of him. Robert Wren notes Nwoye's turn to Christianity as having great importance. Because the community was stressed with its own internal conflicts, "the invader made it possible for the distressed to find relief outside the clan, and in that condition stress became intolerable."[6] The clan thus began to fall apart.

When Nwoye leaves his father's house to join the Christian church, Okonkwo intuits his own end. Kalu Ogbaa writes: "These 'outcasts' were the first to join the new religion . . . Little does he [Okonkwo] realize that the white man's religion offered hopes and brotherhood to the *efulefu*, especially as it stopped the human sacrifice of which his adopted son, Ikemefuna, was a victim."[7]

As Okonkwo disowned Unoka, Nwoye disowns Okonkwo. Nwoye takes the new and symbolic name of Isaac, after the innocent son in the Old Testament who was to be sacrificed by his father Abraham at God's command. Nwoye leaves Mbanta, the motherland, and goes to Umuofia, the fatherland. Donald Weinstock and Cathy Ramadan suggest that by taking the name Isaac, Nwoye is consciously or unconsciously aware "that his father was, like Abraham, willing to sacrifice one son (Ikemefuna, who calls Okonkwo father), and that this latter-day Abraham was still willing, even after that bloody and traumatic event, to sacrifice another son, although in an outwardly different manner."[8]

## Ikemefuna

Ikemefuna is much more like the son Okonkwo wished he had. He becomes a lively, well-liked member of Okonkwo's family, whose presence eases a tension that is always present in the household. Nwoye and Ikemefuna complement each other. Where Nwoye is thoughtful, introverted, and feminine, Ikemefuna is outgoing, adventurous, and masculine. Ikemefuna becomes a catalyst for father and son as Nwoye finds in him a brother who both accepts him and encourages him. Ikemefuna makes Nwoye feel grown up and inspires him to be a man, something Okonkwo could never do. Grateful for the influence Ikemefuna has on his son, Okonkwo becomes more relaxed with Nwoye and easier on him.

# Women

In patriarchal Umuofia, women are good for little more than bearing children and serving the men. Paradoxically, the Igbo greatly value the feminine principle. The earth goddess is most important for the value she imparts to the feminine principle. It is she who gives the people a good crop.

**PARADOX**
When something appears to contradict itself, yet somehow remains true.

# Chielo

The priestess Chielo is a dual character who gives us a glimpse into the religious practices of the clan. She personifies the paradox of finding profound mystery within the ordinary. The only woman with public power in the book, she plays a central role in the community as priestess and oracle of Agbala. When not a priestess, Chielo is an ordinary woman who shares a stand in the market with her friend Ekwefi, Okonkwo's second wife. Interesting to note, Chielo has power only when she becomes the otherworldly, fierce, witch-like figure of a priestess who inspires both fear and obedience. When Chielo speaks, all listen and obey, even Okonkwo.

## Ekwefi

Ekwefi is the only one of Okonkwo's wives we get to know. She and Okonkwo fell in love when they were very young. Too poor to marry her, Okonkwo watched as she became betrothed to another. It was after Okonkwo had acquired a farm and a wife that Ekwefi ran away from her husband and into Okonkwo's house, becoming his second wife. Though he will not show it publicly, Okonkwo has great affection for her.

## Ezinma

Ezinma, daughter of Okonkwo and Ekwefi, is considered to be an *ogbanje*, a child who dies at birth only to be born again. *Ogbanje* children are considered special or gifted in some way. Perhaps that is why Okonkwo cares so much for her, or perhaps it is that she is her mother's child. Although he has children by his other wives, he lacks the strong feeling for them that he does for Ezinma. Ironically, Okonkwo feels that Ezinma is more deserving of his inheritance than his sons. It is she who nourishes Okonkwo's capacity for feeling.

## Obierika

In contrast with Okonkwo is his friend Obierika, a wise, balanced, thoughtful man, much in touch with his *chi*. Where Okonkwo rules his house with a heavy hand, Obierika provides his family with a nourishing environment that inspires growth and culture. This is not to say he is not a tough warrior in a patriarchal society. But, unlike Okonkwo, he understands the necessity for balance and harmony, compromise and flexibility. One might say he is the book's voice of Igbo wisdom and moderation.

Obierika is in touch with his feelings. Okonkwo is not. Obierika is able to find his way around the law without breaking it. Okonkwo cannot. Obierika is more representative of Igbo culture, in that duality is part of his nature. He is able to live comfortably with paradox. Okonkwo cannot. When Okonkwo is exiled, Obierika is among those who burn down his houses and destroy his property. He does not do this to hurt his friend and neighbor. He is simply fulfilling his duty by partaking in the obligatory ritual of appeasing of the earth goddess, a ritual that Joko Sengova compares to "an act of war, albeit aimed at rehabilitating the murderer."[9] Afterwards, Obierika grieves over his friend's loss.

> Why should a man suffer so grievously for an offense he had committed inadvertently? But although he thought for a long time he found no answer. He was merely led into greater complexities. He remembered his wife's twin children, whom he had thrown away. What crime had they committed? The Earth had decreed that they were an offense on the land and must be destroyed.[10]

The wisdom of both Ezeudu and Obierika is lost on Okonkwo. Ezeudu is a wise old man, a titled elder highly respected and highly knowledgeable. Ezeudu warns Okonkwo, "That boy [Ikemefuna] calls you father. Do not bear a hand in his death."[11] When Okonkwo accidentally kills Ezeudu's son at Ezeudu's funeral, the double death might imply Okonkwo's killing of his own earth wisdom, for at this point he is utterly at the mercy of his own unconscious. As Ezeudu was one of Umuofia's great patriarchs, his death and that of his son, who would carry on the tradition, signal the end of an era.

## Uchendu

Uchendu, Okonkwo's uncle, welcomes Okonkwo in exile. When he sees that Okonkwo is depressed, he tells him:

> You think you are the greatest sufferer in the world?
> Do you know that men are sometimes banished for
> life? Do you know that men sometimes lose all their

*yams and even their children? . . . If you think you are*
*the greatest sufferer in the world ask my daughter, Akueni,*
*how many twins she has borne and thrown away?[12]*

Practical and wise, Uchendu points out that
Okonkwo's oversimplification of clan standards
and principles is narrow-minded and unbalanced.
It is Uchendu who explains that "Mother is
Supreme" because it is she who gives comfort
and sympathy.

## The Missionaries

The two missionaries, Mr. Brown and Mr. Smith,
are a pair of opposites. It is perhaps Achebe's own
homage to Igbo balance that he gives us two totally
different representatives of the English colonial
system. Mr. Brown is flexible, levelheaded, and
tolerant. He meets the Igbo on common ground
and is careful not to incur the wrath of the clan.
We sense he is genuine both in his faith and in his
desire to save and convert the Igbo people. His
polar opposite is Mr. Smith, his successor—a
rigid, rash, intolerant racist.

# Achebe's Other Works

## *No Longer at Ease* (1960)

The novel that tells the story of Obi, Okonkwo's grandson, opens with Obi on trial for accepting a bribe. The book then becomes a flashback. Sent by his village to England to get an education, Obi is the first of his people to get a university degree. Full of enthusiasm and idealism, he sails home with high hopes of being an asset to his people. To complicate matters, on the boat home, he has met Clara, who is also from Umuofia. She is, however, an *osu*, who in pre-colonial days were considered outcasts, forbidden to mix with the freeborn in any way. Obi does not consider this a problem as he is a modern educated Nigerian who does not subscribe to the old folkways.

Returning from England, Obi sees Lagos as a rotten wasteland of sewage and dead dogs. The Umuofia Progressive Union holds a reception to welcome him home. When Obi arrives in shirt sleeves because of the heat and gives an unimpressive thank you speech, they are disappointed in him. Where is his black suit and bowler hat? Why is he not dressed in the proper British-inspired manner? After all, he has been granted a post as a civil servant. When he talks idealistically of service to the people rather than white collar jobs and big salaries, they feel betrayed by him and seek to set him straight. He is "their investment which must yield heavy dividends."

The core of the novel is its exploration of greed. The quick and easy getting of money at any cost has virtually displaced the old Igbo ideal of earning money through hard work. Corruption is rampant. Bribery has become a way of life. Like *Things Fall Apart, No Longer at Ease* not only explores the conflict between colonialism and traditional Igbo culture, it reveals the unfortunate effects of the conflict on the individual. Obi is representative of the young educated Nigerian of that time. Traditional cultural identity has been destroyed, yet there is not yet a new cultural and national identity to take its place.

Obi experiences a succession of conflicting demands that challenge his idealism and eventually undermine his integrity. Obi is expected to both pay back his educational loan and to maintain a certain standard of living reflecting his post as a civil servant. Obi struggles both morally and financially. Overburdened with demands, he eventually succumbs to accepting bribes if only to reduce his debt. Troubled by guilt over what he is doing, he decides to reform, but is arrested.

Conflict between Obi's present and his past, moral principles, and his public responsibility is also reflected in his relationship with Clara. The world is not yet ready for such a marriage. Obi's parents, though modern Christians, call on traditional Igbo belief to defend their position against their son marrying Clara, an *osu*. The old ways are not yet dead. As Obi struggles with his own internal dilemma, he becomes a tragic victim caught between two conflicting worlds, each wrestling with internal conflicts of its own.

*No Longer at Ease* takes place in the 1950s, the period during which it was written. The story of Obi was originally intended to be part of *Things Fall Apart*. The main character, Obi, is Nwoye's son and Okonkwo's grandson.

## *Arrow of God* (1964)

*Arrow of God* is the third novel by Chinua Achebe. It takes place in the 1920s by which time colonialism had become firmly established. The main character is Ezeulu, chief priest of Ulu. He is keeper of seasons and names the days of the festival. Ezeulu, who likens himself to the arrow of god, decides what the wishes of the gods are.

Ezeulu finds himself at odds with his own people when he advises them not to go to war with a neighboring village in a land dispute. They reject his advice, and the British quickly put a stop to the fighting. Impressed with Ezeulu, they attempt to set him up as a puppet chieftain in the village. He refuses, however, which gets him arrested and detained by the British administration, thus disrupting his duty as keeper of the calendar of social life. The action makes him popular again for a short time with his own people.

*Arrow of God*, a complex work, shows Christianity as a divisive force in African society. It also explores the problem of personal power that comes from within the self and one's own culture as opposed to invested power that comes from an alien or imposed culture. Parallel to Ezeulu's problem is the struggle with Winterbottom, the district commissioner. Winterbottom is an idealist who strongly believes in the mission of British colonialism. Winterbottom is a man of intelligence and sensitivity, unlike some of the other British on the scene. As he does in *Things Fall Apart*, Achebe sees considerable distinctions in quality of character among the various colonialists as well as the leaders of the Igbo.

## *A Man of the People* (1966)

*Things Fall Apart* looks back to the ordered life that existed within the tribal system just before and during the first days of the British colonial system. *Arrow of God* considers moral and political conflict in Nigeria at the height of British colonial authority. In contrast to those earlier works, *A Man of the People* presents a picture of the new, independent Nigeria that was already deeply steeped in corruption in the mid-1960s, only five years after its independence from Britain.

The main characters are Chief Nanga, the minister of culture, and Odili Samalu the schoolmaster. The two men occupy opposite ends of the political spectrum. Odili has a strict view of public morality as a result of his European style education. At the beginning of the novel, we find him thoroughly disillusioned with the conduct of political affairs in his own country.

Nanga, the politician, is a realist and pragmatist whose main concern is his own political survival. He cares nothing for abstract political theories but knows deep down what the electorate really wants. And what is that? They want, he says, their share of "the national cake." The relationship between the two men offers an opportunity to consider questions of public and private morality in a society that is out of touch with its spiritual past and thinks of the future only in terms of material rewards. The two men find themselves in political conflict and, along the way, Odili sadly comes to realize that the communal power of the village is a vestige of the past.

After Nanga wins the election, Odili challenges him at a victory rally. Odili is attacked and beaten by Nanga's hired thugs and ends up in the hospital with a broken arm and fractured skull. *A Man of the People* ends with a coup staged by the army in reaction to the hopelessly corrupt government installed by Nanga.

The book turned out to be prophetic. The

morning after a meeting of the Society of Nigerian Writers that celebrated the novel's publication, Nigeria experienced its first military coup. The coup had been carried out, as in Achebe's book, with the goal of eliminating the extraordinary corruption of the existing Nigerian government. It eventually failed, an outcome that led to the proclamation in 1967 of the Republic of Biafra and the resulting Nigerian Civil War (1967–1970).

Five years of great turmoil and suffering would pass before Achebe would write again. This time, he published a book of poems relating to the Nigerian Civil War, *Beware Soul Brother* (1971).

## "Anthills of the Savannah"

Another sixteen years would pass before Achebe would publish another novel, *Anthills of the Savannah* in 1987. This novel is also about power struggles and political corruption (this time in a fictional African country named Kangan). It is regarded by many critics as Achebe's best. It tells the story of three schoolmates, friends since childhood, who assume positions of power in a new government. Sam is the president, Chris Oriko is the Commissioner of Information, and Ikem Osidi is the editor of a government-controlled newspaper. Ikem, an idealist and poet, feels very strongly about government reform.

Sam is a selfish leader who has no regard for the people. He only wants to acquire as much power as he can and does not care how he does it. In time, he feels his position threatened by Ikem, and has his friend and former schoolmate murdered. Chris goes into hiding after helping to publicize the truth about Ikem's murder. Critics have noted that in this novel, for the first time, Achebe creates fully developed female characters, and suggests that they are sources of strength and hope in the face of corruption and violence.

## Other Works

Achebe is also the author of collections of short stories, poetry, and several books for juvenile readers. As the director of Heinemann Educational Books in Nigeria, Achebe has encouraged and published the work of dozens of African writers. In 1984 he founded the bilingual magazine *Uwa ndi Igbo*, a valuable source for Igbo studies.

As an essayist Achebe has gained fame with his collections *Morning Yet on Creation Day* (1975), *Hopes and Impediments* (1988), and his book-length essay *The Trouble with Nigeria* (1983) in which he is highly critical of Nigerian political leaders. "The trouble with Nigeria is simply and squarely a failure of leadership. There is nothing basically wrong with the Nigerian character. There is nothing wrong with the Nigerian land or climate or water or air or anything else."[1]

In *An Image of Africa* (1975) Achebe criticizes Joseph Conrad's racism in *Heart of Darkness*. Achebe is also the author of a number of books for children such as *How the Leopard Got His Claws*, *The Drum*, and *The Flute*.

# CHAPTER 9

# African Writers/ African Writing

African writing by black African writers in English, Igbo, or any language scarcely existed before the 1950s, the era which saw the beginning of the breakup of European colonial domination. With it and the appearance of Chinua Achebe and *Things Fall Apart*, 1952 saw the publication of *The Palm-Wine Drinkard* by Amos Tutuola (1920-1997), a Nigerian writer from the Yoruba region of southwestern Nigeria. Tutuola wrote romances and tales of mythical quests, using Yoruba tales and legends and a style in English akin to folk tales. By the 1960s with the coming of independence to many African countries, Achebe and other African writers of fiction in English had turned their attention to the political and social problems that followed.

As Achebe was introducing his highly political *A Man of the People* (1966), Wole Soyinka, another Nigerian writer from the Yoruba region, was publishing *The Interpreters*, a complex work of fiction that has been compared to the work of James Joyce.

Another African writer is Ayi Kwei Armah of Ghana. Armah is the author of *Two Thousand Seasons, Fragments*, and *The Beautiful Ones Are Not Yet Born*. These novels offer a reconstruction and evaluation of the past, and at the same time, a vivid portrait of corruption and moral decay in independent Africa.

The allegorical novel *This Earth, My Brother*, by Kofi Awoonor of Ghana, describes a young man's mental breakdown as a result of moral confusion. Ngugi wa Thiong'o of Kenya became East Africa's major modern novelist. His *Weep Not, Child* is a story of hardship and suffering during Kenya's war for independence.

Chinua Achebe (above) is photographed after receiving the German Booksellers Peace Prize in Frankfurt, Germany, in October 2002.

Black African fiction written in French, from former French colonies such as Cameroon, have dealt with the struggle against colonialism, the search for identity, and conflicts with tyranny after independence. Mongo Bett's Cameroon novel *Ville cruelle* deals with rural Africans in a European-owned logging industry.

Out of South Africa has come Jordan K. Ngubane's novel, *Uvalo Lwezinhlonzi (His Frown Struck Terror)* written in Zulu, followed by his *Ushamba* in English, a work originally banned in South Africa. The first black South African novel to attract international attention was *Mine Boy* by Peter Abrahams. Dennis Brutus is an internationally known South African black poet while Arthur Nortje, another black South African poet, was forced into exile and committed suicide in 1970.

Es'kia Mphahlele became the most widely known of the black South African writers in English. His *Chirundu*, set in Zambia, is in part concerned with two black South African exiles who yearn to return home, even though it means risking police arrest, torture, and imprisonment.

By far, the most important African dramatist to emerge has been Wole Soyinka (1934– ), a Nigerian playwright, poet, novelist, and critic who has created penetratingly powerful yet often satirically comic stage works. Soyinka's *A Dance of the Forest* was commissioned to celebrate Nigerian

independence and was then banned from per-
formance. Soyinka himself, like Achebe and many
African writers (Soyinka and
Achebe are longtime
friends), has had major
difficulties with his own
government. Soyinka was
imprisoned several times for
his criticism of various Nigerian
governments. During the Nigerian Civil War, he
was kept in solitary confinement for two years
because of his presumed support for the Biafran
cause. During the 1970s, he lived for long periods
in exile in France and the United States where,
for a time, he taught at Cornell University.

**SATIRE**
Literary device using
comedy to expose or
make fun of public offi-
cials or negative
societal conditions.

Like his fellow Nigerian activist, Ken Saro-
Wiwa (1941–1995), Soyinka has also criticized the
corruption brought to Nigeria by the oil industry.
Saro-Wiwa, a writer and television producer, was
hanged in 1995 by the Nigerian state for cam-
paigning against the devastation of the Niger Delta
by U.S. oil companies such as Shell and Chevron.

Soyinka, like many other Nigerian writers—including Achebe, John Pepper Clark, and Kole Omotso—was educated at the University College of Ibadan. Like Achebe, Soyinka has been a fervent advocate of African democracy and, in the mid-1970s, campaigned for the overthrow of Idi Amin. In 1986, Soyinka became the first black African writer to win the Nobel Prize for Literature which he dedicated to Nelson Mandela, who was then completing his twenty-third year in a South African prison.

In 1993, Soyinka risked his life and freedom by participating in a protest march against Nigeria's military regime. On a separate occasion, he also witnessed the murder of several other peaceful demonstrators. These events forced Soyinka into exile from Nigeria yet again in 1994, when he once more lived in the United States and France. In 1997 he was tried in absentia (along with fourteen others) and found guilty for alleged terrorist attacks against the Nigerian army. The military regime of General Abacha sentenced

Soyinka to death. "Some people think the Nobel Prize makes you bulletproof. I never had that illusion," Soyinka once said.[1] Following Abacha's death in June 1998, the charge and sentence against Soyinka were dropped. He returned to Nigeria in October 1998.

Back in 1976, Soyinka's best-known essays were published in *Myth, Literature, and the African World.* In this collection, he spoke out against the concept of *négritude*, a philosophy associated with Léopold Senghor, writer and former President of Senegal. *Negritude* emphasizes African consciousness and pride. Soyinka expressed concerns that *négritude* encouraged Africans into a state of cynical self-absorption that was ultimately counter productive. "A tiger does not shout its tigritude," Soyinka argued, "it acts."[2]

*In Things Fall Apart* Achebe does not "shout" the *négritude* of the people of Umuofia, whose story he is telling. In many ways, *Things Fall Apart* is as much a piece of cultural anthropology as it is a work of fiction. It is a balanced living portrait of a civilization and a culture, a way of life that existed for thousands of years before the coming of colonialism. One of the novel's greatest virtues is the extent to which it involves the reader on a human level. In so doing, it breaks down the wall of ignorance and indifference that for so many years separated the average westerner from the so-called "Dark Continent" of Africa.

**1930**— Albert Chinualumogu Achebe (later to be known to the world as Chinua Achebe) is born in the Igbo village of Ogidi in eastern Nigeria, November 16.

**1936**— Starts his education at St. Philip's Central School in Ogidi. By 1938, he is learning English.

**1944**— Enters Government College, Umuahia.

**1948**— Enters University College, Ibadan. Changes his name from the Christian European "Albert" to the Igbo "Chinua."

**1950**— Begins to write stories, essays, and sketches and contributes them to the *University Herald.*

**1953**— Graduates from the University College, Ibadan.

**1954**— Teaches for four months at a small, poorly equipped, rural high school. Is then offered a position as a senior broadcasting officer with the Nigerian Broadcasting Service in Lagos

**1956**— Attends the BBC Staff School in London. Begins writing *Things Fall Apart.* He completes the book in 1957.

**1958**— *Things Fall Apart* is published in London by Heinemann.

**1960**— Nigeria gains its independence from Britain. Achebe wins the Margaret Wrong Prize for the writing of *Things Fall Apart.* His second novel, *No Longer At Ease,* is published.

**1961**— Is appointed director of the *Voice of Nigeria* by the Nigerian Broadcasting Corporation. Marries Christie Chinwe Okoli.

**1962**— First child, a daughter, Chinelo is born, in July.

**1964**— Third novel, *Arrow of God,* is published.

**1966**— Fourth novel, *A Man of the People,* about corruption in post-colonial Nigeria, is published. Immediately after its publication, Nigeria experiences its first military coup. Achebe resigns his job at the Nigerian Broadcasting Corporation and returns to his homeland in Eastern Nigeria.

**1967**—The Eastern Region of Nigeria declares itself an independent state called Biafra. A civil war results that lasts two and a half years (1967–1970) and causes the deaths of a million Igbos. Achebe works tirelessly on behalf of the Biafran cause as he travels to the U.S. and Britain seeking aid for the new distressed nation.

**1970**—Biafra surrenders in January.

**1971**—Begins to write again, and his first book in five years, a volume of poems, *Beware Soul Brother*, is published in Nigeria.

**1972**—Receives his first honorary degree from Dartmouth College in the U.S. He will receive more than thirty others in the next thirty-four years.

**1974**—Begins lecturing at the University of Massachusetts Amherst.

**1975**—Lecture at the University of Massachusetts Amherst on Joseph Conrad's revered classic, *Heart of Darkness*, condemns the book as racist. He accepts an appointment to teach at the University of Connecticut in Storrs.

**1976**—Leaves the University of Connecticut to return to Nigeria where he teaches a course in modern African fiction at the University of Nigeria.

**1983**—Book-length essay, *The Trouble with Nigeria*, which is critical of Nigeria's political leadership, is published in Nigeria, in the U.S., and in Britain.

**1987**—*Anthills of the Savannah*, Achebe's fifth novel and his first in twenty-one years, is published.

**1988**—A Lagos State University award ceremony scheduled to honor Achebe is cancelled because of angry protests against Achebe.

**1989**—Is appointed a Distinguished Professor of English at City College of the City University of New York.

**1990**—Is very seriously injured in an automobile accident on a trip to Nigeria. He is paralyzed from the waist down and is confined to a wheelchair. He accepts an invitation to be a Professor of Literature at Bard College in Annandale, New York.

**2000**—Continues to teach at Bard. He publishes *Home and Exile*, a collection of essays. He celebrates his 70th birthday in a public ceremony at Bard College with Toni Morrison and other African-American writers.

**2004**—Declines to accept the Commander of the Federal Republic (CFR), Nigeria's second highest honor, in protest of the state of affairs in his native country.

**2007**—Continues to teach on the faculty at Bard. He is considered the father of the African novel in English as well as one of the world's most acclaimed writers. *Things Fall Apart* has sold over 10 million copies around the world and has been translated into fifty languages.

# CHAPTER NOTES

## Chapter 1. An African Novel

1. Joyce Cary, *Mister Johnson* (New York: New Directions Books, 1989), p. 99.

2. Ibid., p. 20.

3. Chinua Achebe, *Home and Exile* (New York: Oxford University Press, 2000), pp. 22–23.

4. Ibid., p. 23.

5. Ibid., p. 29.

6. Ibid., p. 21.

7. Ibid., p. 60.

8. Ibid., p. 280.

## Chapter 3. Narrative Style

1. Chinua Achebe, *Things Fall Apart* (New York: Anchor Books, 1994), p. 3.

2. Ibid., p. 16.

3. Ibid., p. 18.

4. Ibid., p. 147.

5. Ibid., p. 13.

6. Walter J. Ong, *Orality and Literacy* (London and New York: Methuen, 1982).

7. William Shakespeare, *Hamlet*, Act III, Scene 1, lines 56–60.

8. Fyodor Dostoyevsky, *Crime and Punishment* (New York: Random House, 1956), p. 320.

9. Achebe, *Things Fall Apart*, p. 153.

10. Ibid.

## Chapter 4. Themes

1. Chinua Achebe, "The Role of the Writer in a New Nation,"

*African Writers on African Writing*, G.D. Killam, ed. (Evanston, Ill.: Northwestern University Press, 1973), p. 8.

2. Simon Gikandi, *Reading Chinua Achebe, Language and Ideology in Fiction* (Portsmouth, N.H.: Heinemann Educational Books, 1993), p. 32.

3. Chinua Achebe, *Things Fall Apart* (New York: Anchor Books, 1994), pp. 5–6.

4. Kalu Ogbaa, *Gods, Oracles, and Divination: Folkways in Chinua Achebe's Novels* (Trenton, N.J.: Africa World Press, 1992), p. 15.

5. Anthonia C. Kalu, "Achebe and Duality in Igbo Thought," *The Literary Griot*, vol. 10, no. 2, Fall, 1998.

6. Achebe, *Things Fall Apart*, p. 11.

7. Ibid., p. 12.

8. Ibid., p. 105.

9. Ibid., p. 46.

## Chapter 5. Literary Devices

1. Kalu Ogbaa, *Understanding Things Fall Apart: A Student Casebook to Issues, Sources, and Historical Documents* (Westport, Conn.: Greenwood Press, 1999), p. 240.

2. Kalu Ogbaa, *Gods, Oracles, and Divination: Folkways in Chinua Achebe's Novels* (Trenton, N.J.: Africa World Press, 1992), pp. 215–216.

3. Chinua Achebe, *Things Fall Apart* (New York: Anchor Books, 1994), p. 41.

4. Ibid.

5. Ibid., p. 48.

6. Ibid.

7. Simon Gikandi, *Reading Chinua Achebe, Language and Ideology in Fiction* (Portsmouth, N.H.: Heinemann Educational Books, 1993), p. 32.

8. Kalu Ogbaa, *Gods, Oracles, and Divination: Folkways in Chinua Achebe's Novels* (Trenton, N.J.: Africa World Press, 1992), p. 111.

9. Achebe, p. 7.

10. Ogbaa, *Gods, Oracles, and Divination*, p. 112.

11. Richard K. Priebe, *Myth, Realism, and the West African Writer* (Trenton, N.J.: Africa World Press, Inc., 1988), pp. 47–48.

12. Achebe, p. 8.

13. Ibid., p. 27.

14. Ibid., p. 26.

15. Ibid., p. 31.

16. Ibid., p. 97.

17. Ibid., p. 75.

18. Ibid., pp. 34–35.

19. Ibid., p. 13.

20. Ibid, p. 51.

21. Ibid., p. 135.

22. Ibid., pp. 118–119.

23. Ibid., p. 175.

24. Ibid., p. 35.

25. Ibid., p. 60.

Chapter 6. Major Characters

1. Chinua Achebe, *Things Fall Apart* (New York: Anchor Books, 1994), pp. 3–4.

2. Ibid., p. 4.

3. Ibid.

4. Neil Kortenaar, "How the Centre Is Made to Hold in *Things Fall Apart*," *Chinua Achebe's Things Fall Apart*, Harold Bloom, ed. (Philadelphia: Chelsea House Publishers, Inc., 2002), p. 84.

5. Solomon Iyasere, "Narrative Techniques in *Things Fall Apart*," *Critical Perspectives on Chinua Achebe*, C.L. Innes and Bernth Lindfors, eds. (Washington, D.C.: Three Continents Press, 1978), p. 100.

6. Achebe, p. 13.

7. Ibid., p. 26.

8. Ibid., p. 28.

9. Ibid., p. 61.

10. Ibid.

11. Ibid., p. 124.

12. Ibid., pp. 133–134.

13. Clement Okafor, "Igbo Cosmology and the Parameters of Individual Accomplishment," Chinua Achebe's *Things Fall Apart*, Harold Bloom, ed. (Philadelphia: Chelsea House Publishers, Inc., 2002), p. 117.

14. Achebe, pp. 182–183.

15. Iyasere, p. 107.

16. Achebe, p. 152.

17. Ibid., pp. 152–153.

18. Ibid., p. 199.

19. Iyasere, p. 107.

20. Achebe, p. 25.

21. Ibid., p. 208.

22. Iyasere, p. 107.

Chapter 7. Minor Characters

1. Simon Gikandi, Reading Chinua Achebe, *Language and Ideology in Fiction* (Portsmouth, N.H.: Heinemann Educational Books, 1993), p. 40.

2. Chinua Achebe, *Things Fall Apart* (New York: Anchor Books, 1994), p. 4.

3. Ibid., pp. 17–18.

4. Ibid., p. 7.

5. Ibid., p. 8.

6. Robert Wren, *Achebe's World: The Historical and Cultural Context of the Novels* (Washington, D.C.: Three Continents Press, 1980), p. 59.

7. Kalu Ogbaa, *Gods, Oracles, and Divination, Folkways in Chinua Achebe's Novels* (Trenton, N.J.: Africa World Press, 1992), p. 34.

8. Donald J. Weinstock and Cathy Ramadan, "Symbolic Structure in *Things Fall Apart,*" *Critical Perspectives on Chinua Achebe*, C.L. Innes and Bernth Lindfors, eds. (Washington, D.C.: Three Continents Press), pp. 132–133.

9. Joko Sengova, "Native Identity and Alienation in Richard Wright's *Native Son* and Chinua Achebe's *Things Fall Apart: A Cross-Cultural Analysis,*" *Mississippi Quarterly*, vol. 1, 50, no. 2, Spring 1997.

10. Achebe, p. 125.

11. Ibid., p. 57.

12. Ibid., p. 135.

## Chapter 8. Achebe's Other Works

1. Chinua Achebe, *The Trouble with Nigeria* (London: Heinemann Educational Books, 1984), p. 1.

## Chapter 9. African Writers/African Writing

1. Wole Soyinka, n.d., <http://www.kirjasto.sci.fi/soyinka.htm> (April 17, 2007).

2. Wole Soyinka, *Myth, Literature, and the African World*, 1976, <http://www.kirjasto.sci.fi/soyinka.htm> (April 17, 2007).

**amnesty**—An act granting a pardon to a group of individuals.

**antipodes**—Any two elements that are directly opposed to one another.

**cliché**—An often repeated phrase, saying, or expression, so often repeated and so common that it is no longer surprising or interesting.

**didactic**—That which is intended to teach a moral point or lesson.

***in absentia***—In the absence of; a person condemned to death in absentia is not usually executed since they are not physically present.

**introverted**—Shy, keeping to oneself, not outgoing.

**irony**—The incongruity of an expected situation (or its outcome) and the actual situation (or its outcome). In language, irony is the deliberate use of words to contrast an apparent meaning with the words' intended meaning (which are usually the complete opposite of each other).

**libation**—A ceremonial drink; the pouring of a liquid as an offering or sacrifice to a God.

**microcosm**—An individual or community seen as a tiny world or universe.

**motif**—A central idea or theme in a literary work.

**myopic**—Only able to see things and situations up close or narrowly; lacking the ability to see the total picture.

**negritude**—A philosophy that preaches a consciousness of and pride in one's African heritage.

*obi*—A house or dwelling.

*ogene*—A Nigerian musical instrument in which bells are struck.

**oracle**—A divinely inspired giver of sacred revelations.

**pantheon**—A temple or high place in which gods or great or notable people are honored.

**paradox**—When something appears to contradict itself, yet somehow remains true.

**patriarchal**—A family, community, or society in which the father is the head of the family and men have authority.

**penury**—Poverty.

**pragmatist**—A person who does things for the purpose of obtaining practical results.

**reparation**—Payment to compensate for injuries or injustices.

**satire**—Literary device using comedy to expose or make fun of public officials or negative societal conditions.

**secular**—Of this world; not pertaining to God or a religion.

**semiotic**—Dealing with signs or symbols.

**synthesis**—A combination of opposing parts or elements.

**theological**—The study of God or religion.

## Novels

*Things Fall Apart* (1958)

*No Longer at Ease* (1960)

*Arrow of God* (1964)

*A Man of the People (1966)*

*Anthills of the Savannah* (1988)

## Short Story Collections

*The Sacrificial Egg and Other Short Stories* (1962)

*Girls at War and Other Stories* (1972)

*African Short Stories* (1985)

## Essays and Lectures

*Morning Yet on Creation Day* (1975)

*The Trouble With Nigeria* (1983)

*Hopes and Impediments, Selected Essays, 1965–87* (1988)

*Home and Exile* (2000)

## Poetry Collections

*Beware, Soul Brother and Other Poems* (1971)

## Children's Books

*Chike and the River* (1966)

*How the Leopard Got His Claws, with John Iroaganachi* (1972)

*The Drum* (1977)

*The Flute* (1977)

**Books**

Bloom, Harold, ed. *Chinua Achebe's* Things Fall Apart. Broomall, Pa.: Chelsea House, 2002.

Njoku, Benedict Chiaka. *The Four Novels of Chinua Achebe: A Critical Study.* New York: Peter Lang Publishing, Inc., 1984.

Ogbaa, Kalu. *Understanding* Things Fall Apart. Westport, Conn.: Greenweood Press, 1999.

Sallah, Tijan M. and Ngozi Okonjo-Iweala. *Chinua Achebe, Teacher of Light: A Biography.* Trenton, New Jersey: Africa World Press, 2003.

**Internet Addresses**

Village of Umuofia
http://www.literaryworlds.wmich.edu/umuofia

Things Fall Apart Study Guide
http://www.wsu.edu:8000/%7Ebrians/anglophone/achebe.html

Postcolonial Literature in Africa
http://www.postcolonialweb.org/misc/africov.html

# INDEX

HBLUW 820
.9009
14
AC4S

Friends of the
Houston Public Library

SHEA, GEORGE.
A READER'S GUIDE TO
CHINUA ACHEBE'S
BLUE RIDGE
05/08